F**K THIS SHIT

F**K THIS SHIT

Sam Dixon

summersdale

When angry, count four;
when very angry, swear.

MARK TWAIN

Must swear off from swearing. Bad habit.

RUTHERFORD B. HAYES

SOD IT

**Fury itself
supplies arms.**

VIRGIL

I long for the
raised voice, the
howl of rage
or love.

LESLIE FIEDLER

SWIVEL ON IT!

Grant me some wild
expressions, Heavens,
or I shall burst.

GEORGE FARQUHAR

!

I wander about
hating everything
I behold.

LORD BYRON

YOU MUST HAVE MISTAKEN ME FOR SOMEONE WHO GIVES A SHIT

If, as we're constantly told,
the world is our oyster, it's
definitely a dodgy one.

DAMIAN BARR

!

Life is a shit sandwich and
every day you take
another bite.

JOE SCHMIDT

TELL IT TO SOMEONE WHO GIVES A FUCK!

Sometimes I wish that I was not supposed to love humanity; the strain is simply too great.

THEODORE DALRYMPLE

!

The only thing that stops God sending a second Flood is that the first one was useless.

NICOLAS CHAMFORT

Sometimes you can get a
splinter even sliding down
a rainbow.

TERRI GUILLEMETS

You common cry of curs!
whose breath I hate
As reek o' the rotten fens,
whose loves I prize
As the dead carcasses of
unburied men
That do corrupt my air...

WILLIAM SHAKESPEARE

WHY MUST EVERYTHING SUCK SO BADLY?

Never go to bed mad.
Stay up and fight.

PHYLLIS DILLER

!

I hate to advocate drugs, alcohol, violence, or insanity to anyone, but they've always worked for me.

HUNTER S. THOMPSON

I was angry with my foe:
I told it not,
my wrath did grow.

WILLIAM BLAKE

!

I don't know, I don't care,
and it doesn't make
any difference.

JACK KEROUAC

ARSEWIPE

I am free of all prejudice.
I hate everyone equally.

W. C. FIELDS

!

**Some days
you're the bug.
Some days you're
the windshield.**

PRICE COBB

ZERO FUCKS GIVEN

Why do you sit there looking like an envelope without any address on it?

MARK TWAIN

!

Your damned nonsense can
I stand twice or once, but
sometimes always,
by God, never.

HANS RICHTER

RIDDLE ME THIS :

WHAT HAS

TWO THUMBS AND

COULDN'T

GIVE A TOSS?

There are days when
it takes all you've
got just to keep up
with the losers.

ROBERT ORBEN

!

I'm tired of this back-slapping
'isn't humanity neat?' bullshit.
We're a virus with shoes, OK?

BILL HICKS

If you can't annoy somebody,
there is little point in writing.

KINGSLEY AMIS

!

If one is not to get into a rage
sometimes, what is the good
of being friends?

GEORGE ELIOT

GREAT STEAMING COWPATS

I like long walks, especially
when they are taken by
people who annoy me.

FRED ALLEN

!

I don't have pet peeves like some people. I have whole kennels of irritation.

WHOOPI GOLDBERG

I don't even want you to nod,
that's how much you annoy me.
Just freeze and shut up.

NEAL STEPHENSON

!

Life is merely terrible.

FRANZ KAFKA

TWATTING

TWAT

TWAT

NO, I JUST LOVE STUPID QUESTIONS, GO FOR YOUR LIFE

Sorrow and shame upon
your head! Ruin upon all
belonging to you!

CHARLES DICKENS

Living with life is very hard.

JEANETTE WINTERSON

SERIOUSLY!?

At times the whole world
seems to be in conspiracy
to importune you with
emphatic trifles.

RALPH WALDO EMERSON

**Other people are
a mistake...**

QUENTIN CRISP

I CAN'T BE DEALING WITH NO FOOLS

Cheer up, the worst is
yet to come.

PHILANDER CHASE JOHNSON

!

The light at the end of the
tunnel is just the light of
an oncoming train.

ROBERT LOWELL

MERDE !!!

Life is just one damned thing after another.

ELBERT HUBBARD

!

There's nothing that cleanses
your soul like getting the
hell kicked out of you.

WOODY HAYES

KEEP AWAY IF YOU

DON'T

LIKE BEING

GROWLED

AT

Since I gave up hope,
I feel so much better.

ANONYMOUS

!

You call me a misanthrope
because I avoid society.
You err; I love society. Yet in
order not to hate people,
I must avoid their company.

CASPAR DAVID FRIEDRICH

BALLS

The truth will set you free. But first, it will piss you off.

GLORIA STEINEM

!

The finest fury is the
most controlled.

CHRISTOPHER HITCHENS

YOU CAN'T EVEN GUESS JUST HOW MUCH I DON'T CARE

Patience provoked often
turns to fury.

PUBLILIUS SYRUS

Life is a four-letter word.

LENNY BRUCE

THANKS A FUCKING LOT

All say, 'How hard it is that
we have to die' - a strange
complaint to come from
the mouths of people who
have had to live.

MARK TWAIN

!

One should forgive
one's enemies,
but not before they
are hanged.

HEINRICH HEINE

BASTARD CRAP

Anger is a signal and one
worth listening to.

HARRIET LERNER

!

It is an immense loss to have all robust and sustaining expletives refined away from one! At such moments of trial refinement is a feeble reed to lean upon.

ALICE JAMES

I SHOULD HAVE STAYED IN BED

Speak when you are angry
and you will make the best
speech you will ever regret.

AMBROSE BIERCE

!

The tigers of wrath
are wiser than the
horses of instruction.

WILLIAM BLAKE

FAN-FUCKING-TASTIC

I shit on the chest of Fun.

HUNTER S. THOMPSON

ARSEHOLES

!

Rage, rage against the dying of the light.

DYLAN THOMAS

DON'T
LET THE
BASTARDS

GRIND YOU DOWN

FUCK THIS
FOR A GAME OF
SOLDIERS

The neurotic has problems,
the psychotic has solutions.

THOMAS SZASZ

!

I don't hate people.
I just feel better when
they aren't around.

CHARLES BUKOWSKI

SHITTING HELL

We must learn how to explode!
Any disease is healthier than
the one provoked by
a hoarded rage.

EMIL CIORAN

I CAN'T BE

ARSED

WITH THIS

!

It is sometimes an
appropriate response
to reality to go insane.

PHILIP K. DICK

BULLSHIT
SATURATION AT
80 PER CENT

When anger walks it is strongest; let it rest and it gets weak.

EDWARD COUNSEL

Oh, isn't life a terrible thing,
thank God?

DYLAN THOMAS

I DON'T GIVE A CRAP

If I had a thunderbolt
in mine eye,
I can tell who should down.

WILLIAM SHAKESPEARE

!

I have always hated crowds.
I like deserts, prisons,
and monasteries.

JEAN GIONO

OH,
SHITBRICKS!

Anger is a great force.
If you control it, it can be
transmuted into a power
which can move the
whole world.

WILLIAM SHENSTONE

!

Man the lifeboats.
The idiots are winning.

CHARLIE BROOKER

DO I LOOK LIKE I CARE?

I know of no more
disagreeable sensation than
to be left feeling generally
angry without anybody in
particular to be angry at.

FRANK MOORE COLBY

!

Take things as they are.
Punch when you have to punch.
Kick when you have to kick.

BRUCE LEE

From hell's heart I stab at thee; for hate's sake I spit my last breath at thee.

HERMAN MELVILLE

!

Come not within the measure
of my wrath.

WILLIAM SHAKESPEARE

FUCK

SHIT

WANK

BOLLOCKS

Life is a sexually transmitted terminal disease.

LEWIS GRIZZARD

!

**No one provokes me
with impunity.**

MOTTO OF THE
ORDER OF THE THISTLE

I COULD TELL YOU HOW I **REALLY** FEEL ...

Life is a gamble at terrible odds - if it was a bet you wouldn't take it.

TOM STOPPARD

!

A man that does not know how
to be angry does not know
how to be good.

HENRY WARD BEECHER

SCHEISSE

Why does the universe go to all the bother of existing?

STEPHEN HAWKING

!

Don't get the impression that you arouse my anger. You see, one can only be angry with those he respects.

RICHARD NIXON

HAPPY BLOODY DAYS

Ninety per cent of everything is crap.

THEODORE STURGEON

!

To be angry is to revenge
the fault of others
upon ourselves.

ALEXANDER POPE

OOHHHHHHHH, BOLLOCKS

There are all these gaps in
speech where you just have
to put a 'fuck'.

NICK HORNBY

!

**If people screw me,
I screw back in spades.**

DONALD TRUMP

DON'T MAKE ME COME OVER THERE...

Away, you scullion! You rampallion! You fustilarian! I'll tickle your catastrophe.

WILLIAM SHAKESPEARE

!

Stupidity is the basic building block of the universe.

FRANK ZAPPA

WHAT A SHITTER

The road to truth is long,
and lined the entire way with
annoying bastards.

ALEXANDER JABLOKOV

!

You have but two topics,
yourself and me, and
I'm sick of both.

SAMUEL JOHNSON

BOLLOCKS TO THIS

Beware the fury of a
patient man.

JOHN DRYDEN

!

My head is quite literally becoming a diseased volcano.

CHARLES BAUDELAIRE

JIZZING HELL

I have love in me the likes
of which you can scarcely
imagine and rage the likes of
which you would not believe.
If I cannot satisfy the one,
I will indulge the other.

MARY SHELLEY

!

To knock a thing down, especially if it is cocked at an arrogant angle, is a deep delight of the blood.

GEORGE SANTAYANA

LIFE'S A BITCH

IS EVERYONE ELSE HEARING WORDS? BECAUSE ALL I'M HEARING IS UTTER, DRIBBLING ARSE-GRAVY

I think it does a man good
to swear.

JEROME K. JEROME

!

Life is short and full
of blisters.

AFRICAN-AMERICAN PROVERB

The steadfastness of the wise is but the art of keeping their agitation locked in their hearts.

FRANÇOIS DE LA ROCHEFOUCAULD

!

A word spoken in
wrath is the
sharpest sword.

SIDDHĀRTHA GAUTAMA BUDDHA

WAKE ME WHEN IT'S OVER

I'll not listen to reason...
Reason always means what
someone else has got to say.

ELIZABETH GASKELL

an optimist is a guy
that has never had
much experience.

DON MARQUIS

ARSE BURGER

Well, of course, people are
only human... But it really does
not seem much for them to be.

IVY COMPTON-BURNETT

!

Moderation in all things. Not too much of life. It often lasts too long.

H. L. MENCKEN

WELL, FUCK A DUCK

I wish I loved the Human Race,
I wish I loved its silly face...
And when I'm introduced to
one, I wish I thought
'what jolly fun!'

WALTER RALEIGH

!

The world is disgracefully managed, one hardly knows to whom to complain.

RONALD FIRBANK

CAUTION:
PISSED-OFF PERSON
AT WORK

What an awful thing life is. It's like soup with lots of hairs floating on the surface.

GUSTAVE FLAUBERT

!

There was something
peculiarly gratifying about
shouting in a blind rage until
your words ran out.

CASSANDRA CLARE

I don't know why we are
here, but I'm pretty sure
that it is not in order
to enjoy ourselves.

LUDWIG WITTGENSTEIN

!

Great anger is more destructive than the sword.

INDIAN PROVERB

ANOTHER FUCKING LOVELY DAY

The art of living is more like
that of wrestling than of
dancing. The main thing is to
stand firm and be ready for
an unforeseen attack.

MARCUS AURELIUS

!

If anger were mileage,
I'd be a very frequent
flyer, right up there
in First Class.

GINA BARRECA

I am much fucking angrier
than you think.

SARAH KANE

!

I am angry nearly every day
of my life.

LOUISA MAY ALCOTT

FUCK THIS SHIT

If you've had a shit day, tell
auntie@summersdale.com and if it's the
shittiest thing we receive that month,
we'll send you something less shit!

See www.summersdale.com/blog/competition
for terms and conditions and all that kind of shit.

Twitter: @Summersdale
www.summersdale.com